creı

MW01294400

BOUNCE HOUSE
RENTAL COMPANY

Tim Roncevich, CISA

Steven Primm, CPA

www.upstartbcg.com

Bounce House Rental Company

Printed in the United States of America

Contents

Introduction

This business plan kit is directly related to your freedom, your personal and financial freedom. Whether you are retired, currently working, or a recent college graduate, this business plan kit provides valuable information for starting a bounce house rental company. This business plan kit is for those individuals who:

- Are passionate about owning a bounce house rental company
- Want a better work/life balance
- Want the flexibility of running their own business
- Want the pride and fulfillment that comes with owning their own business and being an entrepreneur
- Want to earn extra income
- Want to be their own boss

Upstart Business Consulting Group has created this comprehensive business plan kit so you have the tools necessary to pursue your dreams, being an entrepreneur in the United States of America. We only create business plan kits for start-up businesses that can capitalize on current trends based on consumer demand across the United States. All businesses we cover require an initial start-up capital investment of $1,000 to $10,000. Although the required start-up capital is relatively small, you will have the potential for substantial cash flow. The format of this business plan kit is modeled after business plans that have been used in successful start-up companies.

This business plan kit:

- Outlines your business from its creation to the daily operation, all in an easy to understand format
- Was written by successful entrepreneurs and business consultants
- Includes useful information to help you avoid the typical pitfalls that are common in starting your own business
- Includes access to free business templates to help you get your new business started
- Helps you decide on the right legal structure for your new business

- And much more useful information that you need to know when starting your new business

Perhaps the greatest resource this business plan kit provides is the ability for you to e-mail your questions to professional business consultants and entrepreneurs from Upstart Business Consulting Group. Whatever your question may be, you will find a competent resource available to help you.

We know that you will find this business plan kit useful in achieving your goal of personal and financial freedom while building a business you love.

Executive Summary

<u>Company</u>
Your bounce house rental company will be the leader in both client service and in quality equipment. You will focus your efforts on building strategic relationships between party planners, hotel sales and catering managers, banquet facility managers, and local schools. You will offer the highest value bounce house rental experience in your market, allowing controlled and sustainable growth.

<u>Description of Product and Service</u>
Your company will rent high quality equipment to ensure your clients receive the best value in the industry. Equipment will include standard bounce houses, themed jumpers, combo jumpers, and other party equipment (e.g. popcorn popping machines, tables, chairs, snow cone machines etc.). You will have professional, energetic, and knowledgeable staff members to staff the equipment you rent. High quality staff members will ensure proper safety protocols are being followed by your clients.

<u>Market</u>
Bounce houses are more popular than ever, especially among school aged children. If adults are having a party and a large number of children are invited, a bounce house will provide a great source of entertainment. Your bounce house rental company is going to bring this entertainment to your client's front door. Your target market includes parties held at private residences, school events held by all local schools in your target market, and events that were referred to you by 3rd party vendors. Individuals who rent your equipment will be middle to upper class with disposable income. School groups will typically choose the lowest priced quote. This will pose a challenge to you because you will not be the lowest priced bounce house rental company in the market. Clients who were referred to you through word of mouth will choose your company based on your reputation and not price. This will potentially make referrals the most profitable segment of your market.

Financial Profile

Financial projections are based on similar companies in your geographic region. Your price point will be slightly higher than this company. Below is a chart listing key performance indicators for the first three years of operation (based on income statements figures within the business plan):

Key Indicator	Year 1	Year 2	Year 3
Total Revenue	$20,918	$31,378	$47,066
Gross Margin	$14,403	$21,184	$32,166
Operating Income	$11,223	$18,275	$29,257
Net Income	$7,407	$12,062	$19,310

Funds Needed and Use of Proceeds

Your bounce house rental company will need $10,000 in startup funding. Funding will consist of personal savings from the owner/s. The proceeds will be used to pay for equipment, a truck or trailer to house the equipment, insurance, and marketing expenditures. Future growth will be funded through the company's positive cash flow or through the use of credit cards. Additional capital from new investors will not be used due to the high cost associated with this type of financing.

Summary Description of the Business

Mission Statement

A mission statement formally declares what your company is trying to achieve in the medium to long term. Your mission statement should be market oriented and defined by your product or service (e.g. "We rent bounce houses"). You should avoid making your mission too narrow or too broad. Your mission should be realistic and should not be used for public relations purposes, but instead be specific with workable guidelines. A good market oriented mission statement should sound like this: "We create excitement by offering our clients the highest quality bounce houses coupled with our knowledgeable and friendly staff. We strive to become the provider of choice for bounce house equipment within the Acme County area."

Business Model

The business model defines how you plan to execute your mission statement. Your company needs to provide the highest quality bounce houses along with the friendliest and most knowledgeable staff in your target market. Since you may have competition in the area, the combination of quality equipment and great staff will enable long term growth and success.

Strategy

The strategy of your bounce house rental company should consist of the following:

- Attract profitable clients who value the quality of service that you provide. Do not try to win new business by being the low price leader. Charge a fair price and emphasize your quality service and quality equipment.
- Provide the highest bounce house value to your clients. This means providing the highest quality service at a price clients are willing to pay. Do not try to "nickel and dime" your clients for short term profit. Instead, focus on pleasing the client to ensure a long term relationship and positive word of mouth. This type of strategy will enable long term growth and higher profit margins.

- Grow the business in a smart way. Before spending too much money through purchasing bounce houses and other equipment, be sure there will not be cash flow restraints that may be harmful to the business. If possible, employ bootstrap financing. Bootstrap financing is a collection of finance methods used to minimize the amount of outside debt and equity financing needed from banks and investors. Bootstrap financing requires the entrepreneur to start the business with as little capital as possible early in the life of the business in order to generate positive cash flow as soon as possible. Bootstrap financing methods include personal savings, credit cards, second mortgages, and friends/family.
- Network and create key contacts within the party planning industry. Create a commission structure of 5% to 10% of individual party revenue to create an incentive for party planners to refer business to your company.
- Build the business through word of mouth referrals. Word of mouth is the passing of information by verbal means, especially recommendations, in an informal, person-to-person manner. Word of mouth is not only the most credible form of marketing, but it is also the least expensive. Subscribe to the Word of Mouth Marketing newsletter to gain insight on word of mouth marketing techniques (*www.womma.org*).

When properly applied, the above business strategy should allow for sustained growth and early positive cash flow to fund future growth.

Strategic Relationships
Strategic relationships should consist of the following individuals and groups:
- Party Planners: party planners would not be in business if they did not have high quality vendors to choose from to outsource work. You should build the relationship to become the preferred bounce house vendor for party planners. A 5% to 10% commission is also a great incentive to entice party planners to use your company. When a party planner does use your service, you must fulfill your promise of providing the

highest level of service to ensure the relationship between the party planner and your company endures.

- Previous Clients: past clients provide the most credible word of mouth. Continually build the relationship with your clients, preferably by e-mail or telephone. Send cards for client birthdays, anniversaries, or just to say hello. Cards are also an effective way to notify past clients about your upcoming promotions.

- Hotel Sales and Catering Managers: hotel sales and catering managers build their business through repeat clients. If you provide high quality service at a fair price, the hotel sales and catering managers will have satisfied clients. With satisfied clients, the hotel sales and catering managers will be extremely pleased because they have worked hard to build the relationship with their clients. Providing high quality service should make you the preferred bounce house vendor. Additionally, a 5% to 10% commission is also a great incentive to entice hotel sales and catering managers to use your company. Although the hotel sales and catering managers may not be able to accept a commission due to a conflict of interest, it is always best to offer the incentive as goodwill.

- Banquet Facility Managers: just like hotel sales and catering manager, banquet facility managers build their business by repeat clients. If you provide high quality service at a fair price, the banquet facility managers will have satisfied clients. With satisfied clients, the banquet facility managers will be extremely pleased because they have worked hard to build the relationship with their clients. Providing high quality service should make you the preferred bounce house vendor. Additionally, a 5% to 10% commission is also a great incentive to entice banquet facility managers to use your company. Although the banquet facility managers may not be able to accept a commission due to a conflict of interest, it is always best to offer the incentive as goodwill

- Local Schools: bounce houses are a great source of entertainment for school children (from elementary school through high school). Network with the Activities Director, or whoever makes planning decisions for school activities, at every local school. Since schools have a limited budget for entertainment, you may want to charge a very competitive price to ensure your company is chosen whenever the school needs a bounce house. This will help build a long term relationship, which means strong word of mouth marketing and long term growth.

- Party Referral Websites and Business Directories: this may be the fastest way to build your business. A party referral website is great because everyone who browses the website is specifically looking to rent a bounce house for their event. Such websites include partypop.com, superpages.com, and yellowpages.com.

SWOT Analysis

The SWOT Analysis is used to identify your company's Strengths, Weaknesses, Opportunities, and Threats in order to identify a strategic niche that your company can exploit. By understanding these components and how they apply to your business, you should be able to improve operations and strategies in many areas to grow and sustain your profitability. We recommend you complete a SWOT analysis every 12-18 months. Below is a sample SWOT analysis that you can use to guide your own SWOT analysis:

Strengths:
- High quality bounce houses. You will purchase commercial grade bounce houses because they are more durable and safer than less expensive bounce houses that are designed for light home use.
- You will create strategic relationships with party planners, hotels sales and catering managers, school Activities Directors, and banquet facility managers. These strategic relationships will lead to repeat business and sustained long term growth

Weaknesses:
- Do not have established reputation in the party rental industry.
- Entrenched competitors with established brand and client base may have a large percentage of the market (see "*Opportunities*" section below).

- Low barriers to entry include low start up capital and new competitors with a large network who can easily sell bounce houses to their existing network.

Opportunities:
- If there is a large competitor, you have the opportunity to come in and take market share. Your unique combination of high quality bounce houses and great client service will create raving clients who will generate positive word of mouth.
- Positive cash flow can be expected after the first several events.
- The popularity of bounce houses is increasing and the demand for this service is growing.
- Low cost, entry level business for the upstart entrepreneur. You will need about $10,000 to start the business.

Threats:
- Growth may be rapid, but must be controlled. Do not purchase equipment until you have booked a party that requires extra equipment. Avoid excess inventory by not buying bounce houses that have no demand.
- New competition undercuts your prices. However, if you create a strong client base and solid word of mouth of marketing, you will not have to worry about your clients going with another company for a lower price. Trust breeds loyalty, and loyal clients are great for long term growth. Client loyalty is what separates successful companies from unsuccessful companies.

Product and Service

Product Process
High quality equipment including:
- Standard bounce houses
- Themed jumpers
- Combo jumpers
- Slide jumpers
- Velcro wall jumpers
- Bungee runs
- Sumo suits
- Party Extras
    - Folding tables (length of tables vary from 4' to 10')
    - Folding chairs
    - Popcorn popping machines
    - Table tennis tables
    - Cotton candy machines
    - Snow cone machines
    - Plus other types of equipment that you find your clients want to rent

Service Process
Professional, energetic, and knowledgeable staff members create raving clients. A staff member is usually not required at private residences who rent a single bounce house. However, some events will rent multiple bounce houses or inflatables that require supervision. If you rent multiple bounce houses or inflatables that require supervision (e.g. a basketball hoop shot inflatable or a Velcro wall jumper), you want a staff member onsite to supervise the inflatables and make sure safety protocols are being followed,

High quality service will determine if your company will be successful or unsuccessful. It does not matter how nice your bounce houses look, service is by far the most important element of your business strategy. In order to attract quality staff, you will have to pay a decent wage. Wages should range from $40 to $50 per event (up to 4 hours), depending on what inflatable your staff members are supervising. This wage range will attract staff members who are more professional

17

and friendly than if you paid less. Staff members should be paid on a "per event" basis to qualify them as independent contractors (refer to the "Inflatable Attendant" section for additional information).

Location

A bounce house rental company is the perfect home based business. We highly recommend you use a home office to run your business, not only for the tax benefits, but also for the overhead cost savings. The majority of the equipment should be housed in your company truck or trailer. Excess equipment can be housed in your garage. If you have any local ordinances that prevent you from storing the truck or trailer in your driveway, you can rent a parking space at your local storage facility for a small monthly fee.

Legal Structure

Type of Legal Structure
Below is a brief description of the major types of legal structures you may choose to form. Following the description, there will be a handy chart that will give you a brief snapshot of the pros, cons, and tax rules for each legal structure.

- Sole Proprietorship: A sole proprietorship is a one person business that is not registered with the state. You do not have to do anything special or file any papers to set up a sole proprietorship. You create a sole proprietorship just by going into business for yourself. Legally, a sole proprietorship is inseparable from its owner (i.e. the business and the owner are one and the same). This means the owner of the business reports business income and losses on his or her personal tax return and is personally liable for any business related obligations, such as debts or court judgments. Your income tax return for this business is filed on Schedule C of your individual form 1040. Self-employment taxes (i.e. the employer and employee's share of FICA taxes) are to be paid upon all earnings from a sole proprietorship in addition to standard income taxes. If your business operates under a trade name (e.g. Fly High Bounce Houses), you must file a fictitious business name registration with the county in which you will be operating. However, there will be no state franchise taxes due. In California, for example, the minimum annual franchise tax for corporations is $800 per year. However, most other states have annual franchise taxes under $100. Refer to your state franchise tax board for additional information.

  Sole proprietorships make sense in a business where personal liability is not a big worry (e.g. a small service business in which you are unlikely to be sued and for which you will not be borrowing much money for inventory or other costs).

- Partnership: A partnership is simply a business owned by two or more people that has not filed papers to become a corporation or a limited liability company (LLC). You do not have to file any paperwork to form a partnership. The partnership arrangement begins as soon as you start a business with another person. As in a sole proprietorship, the partnership's owners pay taxes on their share of the business income on their personal tax returns. Partners are each personally liable for the entire amount of any business debts and claims. Also, each partner has the potential to hold all partners liable for actions taken in connection with the business. To avoid future feuds and confusion, a partnership should have a written partnership agreement that spells out the rights and duties of the partners relative to partnership assets, liabilities, income (loss), and control of business operations. Refer to the sample partnership agreement on the template page of the UBCG website. Partnerships file a separate tax return on federal form 1041 and partners pay Social Security and Medicare on all partnership earnings.

Partnerships make sense in a business where personal liability is not a big worry (e.g. a small service business in which you and your partners are unlikely to be sued and for which you will not be borrowing much money for inventory or other costs).

- Limited Liability Company (LLC): An LLC is formed through the filing of articles of organization with the appropriate state office for corporate filings (usually the Secretary of State). An LLC is a hybrid between a partnership and a corporation. Generally, LLC's are required by state law to have written operating agreements that set forth the rights and duties of the LLC members, much like a partnership agreement. Refer to the sample LLC operating agreement on the template page of the UBCG website. Although an LLC can be organized with non-member managers operating the business, the IRS has ruled that in most cases LLC members shall be liable for self-employment taxes on their share of LLC earnings. An LLC reports its income (loss) on federal form 1041. LLC members are not personally liable for the debt of an LLC. LLC's provide limited personal liability for business debts and claims.

But when it comes to taxes, LLC's are more like partnerships (i.e. the owners of an LLC pay taxes on their share of the business income on their personal tax returns). The main benefit of an LLC is that these structures limit the owners' personal liability for business debts and court judgments against the business.

LLC's make sense for business owners who either 1) run the risk of being sued by clients, 2) run the risk of piling up a lot of business debt, or 3) have substantial personal assets they want to protect from business creditors.

- S-Corporation: A corporation is formed through the filing of articles of incorporation with the state. Refer to the sample articles of incorporation on the template page of the UBCG website. There is no distinction between an S-Corporation and a C-Corporation when the initial filing of the articles of incorporation is made with the state. To become an S-Corporation, a corporation must file Form 2553 with the IRS within a certain deadline to qualify for S status. If you fail to make a timely S-Corporation election, the corporation is automatically a C-Corporation. S-Corporations are taxed on income (and losses) like partnerships in that there is no entity level taxation. Please note that S-Corporations that formerly were C-Corporations can be taxed upon "built-in gains" that existed upon their conversion from C to S. Shareholders are not personally liable for the debts of S-Corporations. Employment and unemployment taxes are only paid upon the designated salary of a shareholder and not upon dividends. What sets an S-Corporation apart from all other types of businesses is that an S-Corporation is an independent legal and tax entity, separate from the people who own, control, and manage it. Because of this separate status, the owners of an S-Corporation do not use their personal tax returns to pay taxes on corporate profits. Instead, the S-Corporation itself pays these taxes. Owners pay personal income tax only on money they draw from the corporation in the form of salaries and bonuses. The main benefit of an S-Corporation is that these structures limit the owners' personal liability for business debts and court judgments against the business.

An S-Corporation makes sense for business owners who either 1) run the risk of being sued by clients, 2) run the risk of piling up a lot of business debt, or 3) have substantial personal assets they want to protect from business creditors.

- C-Corporation: A corporation is formed through the filing of articles of incorporation with the state. Refer to the sample articles of incorporation on the template page of the UBCG website. There is no distinction between an S-Corporation and a C-Corporation when the initial filing of the articles of incorporation is made with the state. If you fail to make a timely S election, the corporation is automatically a C-Corporation. C-Corporations have their income taxed at the corporate level. S-Corporations that formerly were C-Corporations can be taxed upon "built-in gains" that existed upon their conversion from C to S. Shareholders are not personally liable for the debts of C-Corporations. Employment and unemployment taxes are only paid upon the designated salary of a shareholder and not upon dividends. What sets the C-Corporation apart from all other types of businesses is that a C-Corporation is an independent legal and tax entity, separate from the people who own, control and manage it. Because of this separate status, the owners of a C-Corporation do not use their personal tax returns to pay tax on corporate profits. Instead, the C-Corporation itself pays these taxes. Owners pay personal income tax only on money they draw from the corporation in the form of salaries and bonuses. The main benefit of a C-Corporation is that these structures limit the owners' personal liability for business debts and court judgments against the business.

A C-Corporation makes sense for business owners who either 1) run the risk of being sued by clients, 2) run the risk of piling up a lot of business debt, or 3) have substantial personal assets they want to protect from business creditors.

Type of Structure	Pros	Cons	Tax Rules
Sole Proprietorship	Simple and inexpensive to create and operate	Owner personally liable for business debts and lawsuits	Owner reports profit or loss on his or her personal tax return (schedule C of form 1040)
General Partnership	Simple and inexpensive to create and operate	Owners (partners) personally liable for business debts and lawsuits	Entity must file form 1065. Each partner receives a Schedule K with their proportion of income and expenses which is included with each individual's income tax return (form 1040)
Limited Liability Company (LLC)	Owners have limited personal liability for business debts even if they participate in management	More expensive to create than partnership or sole proprietorship State laws for creating LLC's may not reflect latest federal tax changes	Profit and loss can be allocated differently than ownership interests IRS rules now allow LLC's to choose between being taxed as a partnership or a corporation
C-Corporation and S-Corporation	Owners have limited personal liability for business debts Fringe benefits limited for owners who own more than 2% of shares	More expensive to create than partnership or sole proprietorship More paperwork than a Limited Liability Company (LLC), which offers similar advantages	Owners report their share of corporate profit or loss on their personal tax returns Owners can use corporate loss to offset income from other sources. Income must be allocated to owners according to their ownership interests

Choosing a Legal Structure

Most owners of bounce house rental companies will operate as a sole proprietorship or general partnership. These are the easiest and least expensive to form and tax filings are relatively simple. Limited liability companies are designed for businesses that expect to be sued from time to time and the owners want to protect their personal assets. As all individual situations are different, professional tax and legal advice is recommended if you are not sure which legal structure is right for you.

List of Owners and/or Corporate Officers

This section should list owners and how profits, losses, and expenses will be distributed. Include a list of each owner's strengths along with resumes as an appendix to the business plan. Depending on the legal structure of your company, you will need to create a partnership agreement, articles of incorporation, or LLC operating agreement. Refer to the "Type of Legal Structure" section for additional details.

Name	Title	Responsibilities	Owner (Yes/No)	Ownership % (Partnerships only)

Management

List of Key Managers

This section should list key management personnel who will be running the business. Include a list of the manager's strengths along with resumes as an appendix to the business plan.

Manager Responsibilities

Since a bounce house rental company is a great home-based business, we recommend you only hire managers to work on the day of the event. As the business owner, you should be booking equipment, booking staff members to supervise the bounce houses, and answering client questions. If you have a manager perform all of these tasks, then you risk them taking this knowledge and starting their own bounce house rental company (refer to the low barriers to entry weakness in the "SWOT Analysis" section). Your manager should handle the following "day of" responsibilities:

- Picking up equipment from your home or trailer storage yard.
- Delivering, setting up, and breaking down all equipment required for each event.
- Being the onsite point of contact for your company (for large events only). Be sure to tell your client that you will not be onsite the day of the event but will have a capable manager onsite to handle the event.
- Managing staff members as they arrive to ensure they are wearing the proper.
- Collecting all outstanding payments that are owed to your company.

Manager Salaries

You may choose to pay your managers a set hourly wage or base their pay off of a percentage of revenue or profit for each party. You should discuss the options with your managers and decide which form of wage calculation they would prefer. With a set hourly wage, you can easily estimate how much your manager will make each night. However, for smaller parties, you may end up paying your managers a disproportionate amount of money for the work they are performing. With the percentage of revenue or profit type of wage, your managers will end up making more for larger events (which are more complex to manage and require more effort) and less on smaller events (which are easier to manager and require less effort).

Personnel

<u>Inflatable Attendant (staff member)</u>
Inflatable Attendants should be independent contractors. The independent contractor relationship benefits both you and the Inflatable Attendants. However, you become liable for all withholding taxes and possible nonpayment penalties if the IRS reclassifies your Inflatable Attendants as employees and not independent contractors. As a company that only hires independent contractors, you have less paperwork and are not required to do the following:

- Provide the same fringe benefits offered to employees, such as insurance coverage, vacation days, sick days, and pensions.
- Pay unemployment taxes.
- Pay half of the FICA tax.
- Pay other state and local taxes, such as unemployment and workers compensation.
- Withhold income taxes and Social Security taxes (FICA) from employee wages.

Additionally, as independent contractors, your Inflatable Attendants receive the tax benefits of a self-employed businessperson, such as travel and entertainment deductions. No taxes are withheld from the earnings of independent contractors because they are responsible for the payment of their own taxes. Remember, you must complete Form 1099-MISC for all your dealers.

The main factors that distinguish an independent contractor from an employee are whether the employer "controls" the worker and the basis upon which the worker is paid. Independent contractors are those who:

- Are paid on a commission or per-job basis (not an hourly wage).
- Do not submit oral or written reports.
- Set their own pace and the sequence of services performed.
- Pay for their own traveling expenses.
- Furnish their own tools and materials (e.g. attire).
- Provide services to the general public.
- Cannot be fired if contract specifications are met.

- Work for more than one employer or, at the very least, are not required to work full-time for one employer.
- Are hired to perform one particular job at a time and do not work for the same employer year after year.
- Do not receive any job training from the employer.
- Work on their own and decide how work is to be completed without employer direction.

If you are in doubt whether your Inflatable Attendants are employees or independent contractors, file Form SS-8 ("Information for Use in Determining Whether a Worker Is an Employee for Purposes of Federal Employment Taxes and Income Tax Withholding") with the IRS. Either way, make sure to take the following precautions to prevent an unfavorable audit from the IRS:
- The worker should bill you for services rendered.
- Draft a written contract that provides for and/or contains (1) the type of service to be performed, (2) the place of work, (3) payment, (4) duration of the contract, (5) an arbitration clause, and (6) a covenant against competition.
- As much independence as possible should be given to the worker (e.g. supervision on the job or the location where the work is to be performed).
- The worker should be required to provide his or her own tools, supplies, training, and transportation.

The IRS may see your managers as employees if you pay them hourly or have to much "control" over the work they complete. In order to have your managers be seen as independent contractors, you may decide to pay them on a per job basis (e.g. percentage of revenue or profit for each event) and follow the above guidelines and precautions. Remember, having independent contractors will increase your bottom line due to the significant tax savings.

Necessary Qualifications
You need to identify the necessary qualifications that you will be looking for when hiring employees or independent contractors. You need to identify these qualifications through the use of job descriptions. At a minimum, you will need job descriptions for the

following positions that are considered critical for a bounce house rental company:

- Sales and Client Service Representative: job responsibilities include being the main point of contact for your company. This person should book all events and field all client questions before the event occurs. Also, this person should contact the client after the event to ensure all expectations were met. Job responsibilities should be completed by company owner.
- Delivery, Setup, and Breakdown Crew: job responsibilities include delivering, setting up, and breaking down all bounce house equipment at the event site. Job responsibilities can be combined with the Event Manager position and can be performed by company owner or manager.
- Inflatable Attendant Staffer: job responsibilities include hiring Inflatable Attendants and maintaining a current Inflatable Attendant list. When an event is booked, the Inflatable Attendant Staffer will send out the event inquiry (preferably via e-mail) to all Inflatable Attendants and book those who respond to the event inquiry. Job responsibilities should be completed by the company owner.
- Event Manager: job responsibilities include managing the "day of" details of the event. This person will be the face of your company and will be responsible for ensuring the event runs smoothly and successfully. Job responsibilities can be combined with the Delivery, Setup, and Breakdown Crew position and can be performed by company owner or manager.
- Inflatable Attendant: job responsibilities include assisting clients with the inflatables and ensuring all clients are adhering to all safety protocols. Inflatable Attendants are tasked with providing great service to your clients. Job responsibilities can be performed by independent contractors. Also, the Event Manager and owners should be able to perform the tasks of the Inflatable Attendant.

Job Descriptions

Job descriptions should include the following information:

- Job Title
- Direct Report (who the worker is supposed to report to)

- General Summary
- Essential Duties and Responsibilities
- Job Specifications and Requirements
- Qualifications
- Experience
- Working Conditions
- Disclaimer (e.g. "The above statements are intended to describe the general nature and level of work being performed by people assigned to this classification. They are not intended to be construed as an exhaustive list of all responsibilities, duties, and skills required of personnel so classified")
- Approved By
- Approval Date
- Refer to the sample job description on the template page of the UBCG website.

Expected Hours
- Sales and Client Service Representative: hours per week varies based on the demand for events. Active marketing and sales should require at least 15 hours per week. Each event you have booked will require approximately 1-2 hours of client relations and answering questions.
- Delivery, Setup, and Breakdown Crew: 6 hours for each event. The crew should arrive to pickup equipment 1 hour prior to events start time (allows time to drive to the event and setup the equipment), work the event for 4 hours (if necessary), and 1 hour for cleanup and to return the equipment.
- Inflatable Attendant Staffer: depending on the size of the event, it may take anywhere between 5 minutes and 2 hours to fill all staff positions. We recommend you maintain an e-mail database containing all Inflatable Attendant e-mail addresses. Therefore, when you have an event, all the Inflatable Attendant Staffer must do is send a mass e-mail to all of your Inflatable Attendants and fill the spots on a first come, first served basis. This will make the Inflatable Attendant Staffer's job easy as well as provide a consistent way for your Inflatable Attendants to reply to event inquiries.

- Event Manager: if this person is not the same person as the "Delivery, Setup, and Breakdown Crew", then expect to spend 5 hours at the event. The Event Manager should arrive 30 minutes prior to the event to meet the client, manage the 4 hour event, and stay 30 minutes after the event to ensure the client is satisfied with the night.
- Inflatable Attendant: Inflatable Attendants should be contracted for 4 hours. Pay should be based off 4 hours of work, even if the event is scheduled for less than 4 hours. Since you should be renting the equipment based on 4 hours of service, the Inflatable Attendant cost is already built in to the price structure. You should always book events for 4 hours to keep your price consistent. Inconsistency in pricing will confuse your clients and inconsistency in payments to Inflatable Attendants will confuse them, which may turn them off from working for your company in the future.

Future Needs to Adding Employees and Independent Contractors
As your business grows, you will need additional Inflatable Attendants to fill available positions. You should never stop trying to attract new Inflatable Attendants. The best way to attract new Inflatable Attendants is to ask current Inflatable Attendants if they can refer any friends. You can also post flyers at local college campuses, post advertisements in a local newspaper, or post advertisements on the web (e.g. Craigslist). However, when you post advertisements in newspapers and on websites, be ready to expect a high number of responses. Unfortunately, you will only have a few quality leads. There will be many people interested in the position, but you may end up having only 3% of the original leads stay on as consistent Inflatable Attendants.

Accounting Software

Accounting for your business is a vital activity to ensure your long term success. Accurate and diligent accounting of your income and expenses will ensure you have collected past due balances from your clients and are prepared to easily file your tax return at the end of the year. Spreadsheets are helpful and the use of special accounting software makes accounting a breeze. User-friendly software, such as QuickBooks, will provide all the accounting activities and services most businesses will need. Accounting software is also easy to import into tax software (e.g. Turbo Tax). Although there are companies that provide accounting services, keeping track of your own accounting activities will allow you to keep more of your hard earned income in your own pocket.

Legal

Your company should seek legal representation on an as needed basis. For general legal questions, you may be able to rely on a friend who is an attorney. For tax-based legal questions, you can ask a Certified Public Accountant (CPA) for assistance. Before you pay an attorney, consult with your local Service Corp of Retired Executives (SCORE) counselor or local Small Business Administration (SBA) office to see if one of their consultants can answer your question at no charge. You can contact SCORE and the SBA through their respective websites (www.score.org and www.sba.gov).

Insurance

There are at least three types of insurance that are recommended for this type of business:

- Truck and/or Trailer Insurance: you will need both liability and replacement coverage for your business truck and/or trailer.
- Content Insurance: if the truck or trailer is stolen or the equipment that is stored within the truck or trailer is damaged, you will need this insurance to recover the cost of the equipment.
- $1,000,000 General Liability Insurance: you will need this insurance to protect you from injuries that your independent contractors or clients suffer at your events. Additionally, some facilities require you to have insurance when hosting events at their location.

Consult with your current insurance provider to obtain quotes. Remember, before you choose coverage, shop around with other insurance brokers to find the best price. As your business grows and you acquire additional assets, consult with your insurance provider to determine if you need additional insurance coverage.

Security

Depending on how much equipment you buy, you may be able to store all of it in your business truck and/or trailer. Excess equipment that does not fit in your business truck and/or trailer can be stored in your garage. You may have up to $50,000 worth of equipment as your business grows, so you want to make sure your investment is secure. Whether your equipment is stored in your business truck and/or trailer or your garage, security must be of the utmost importance. Make sure your equipment remains behind locked doors at all times. If you store your equipment at a public storage facility, be cognizant of your surroundings. If you store your equipment in your garage or keep your business truck and/or trailer on your own property, consider purchasing a security camera to record the area of your property where you store the equipment. Security cameras can be purchased from your local warehouse store, electronics store, or a store specializing in security. Preventative measures like a security camera deter potential thieves. Especially with security, an ounce of prevention is worth a pound of cure.

Overview and Goals of Marketing Strategy

If implemented properly, your marketing strategy should allow for sustained and controlled growth. The next four sections detail the key elements of your marketing strategy.

Market Analysis

<u>Target Market</u>
Your target market consists of the following types of groups:
- Events for individuals at their residences:
    - o If the interested client was referred to you by a previous client, chances are they will be more concerned with quality service and quality equipment and less concerned about price. You can typically charge full price for these types of clients.
    - o If the interested client found your company through your other advertising methods (e.g. online ad, yellow pages, etc.), chances are they have contacted several other bounce house rental companies for quotes. These clients tend to be more price sensitive and may look for the lowest priced company. Explain to these clients that the price is based on the high level of service and the high quality inflatables you provide. Try to convince them that even though you charge a higher price than your competitors, your clients receive a much higher level of service. If they refuse to pay your price, you may want to drop your price slightly as a sign of goodwill and to gain the business. However, do not drop your price too much because you end up losing the high quality service image that will make your company a long term success.
- Events that were referred to you by a 3rd party vendor: if the interested client was referred to you by a party planner, chances are they will be more concerned with quality service and quality equipment and less concerned about price. You can typically charge full price for these types of clients. If you exceed expectations, you will not only receive future business from the client, but you will also receive future referrals from the party planner. You can build your business very fast if you have a large network of party planners that refer all bounce house events your way. If you give commissions to party planners, a good tip is to add the party planner commission to the price of the party. This will allow you to pass the

commission expense on to the client and retain your normal profit margin.
- Events for schools: school groups are typically looking for the lowest priced service provider. Since schools have a limited budget for entertainment, you may want to charge a very competitive price to ensure your company is chosen whenever the school needs a bounce house. You can afford to offer a lower price because you will likely be contracted out for 3-4 events per year. The benefits gained from the volume of events you hold at schools outweigh the lower profit margin of each event.

Competition

You must know who your competitors are and what they are charging for their service. The easiest way to identify competition is by using search engines on the internet as well as looking through the local yellow pages. Once you find out who your competitors are, you must perform market research. Market research is best conducted by calling your competitors and saying you are planning on renting bounce houses and other inflatables and you need quotes. Obtain several quotes for multiple packages so you get an idea of how much they are charging. Once you have a full list of competitors, describe their strengths and weaknesses and compare them to your company. This will be important when you are explaining to clients what sets your company apart from your competition. Remember, be close to your friends and be even closer to your enemies. We suggest you repeat this process every 6 months to identify new competition and to ensure your pricing strategy remains competitive.

Market Trends

You must identify industry trends (for the party equipment rental industry) and client trends (see "*Target Market*" section above) every 6 months to ensure you are providing the right equipment and are charging a fair price. Additionally, you need to take into account economic trends to determine if you can increase your price or if you need to decrease your price to become more competitive in the market.

Market Research

Market research can be completed through the following methods:

- Internet: use search engines to find the websites of your competitors. Identify how your competitors are advertising, what equipment they are providing, and how much they charge. Browse the websites of your competitors and identify what you like and what you dislike. When designing your website, make sure it looks professional because this will likely be the first way potential clients research your company and determine if they want to call you for a quote. We suggest you hire a professional web designer to make sure your website looks as professional as possible. Make sure the web designer maximizes your website's exposure to internet search engines. You want to ensure your company is as visible as possible to potential clients who are conducting online research for bounce house rental companies in your geographic region.
- Yellow Pages: use the Yellow Pages to see which competitors are advertising in print. Based on the potential return on investment, you must determine if you want to advertise via the yellow pages or spend your advertising dollars elsewhere.
- Friends and Family: ask your friends and family members what they would want if they were looking for a bounce house rental company. Ask if they are more concerned with high quality equipment and a high level of service or if they are more concerned in paying a low price. Ask at least 10 friends and family members to make sure you have a broad amount of market research to base your conclusions.
- Party Planners: ask various party and event planners who they use for bounce house rental services and how much they pay. Ask why they use their current service provider and if they will be willing to refer business to your company.

Marketing Strategy

General Description
Your marketing strategy should be tailored to your individual marketing strengths. Your marketing strategy should support your overall business strategy that was stated earlier under the "Summary Description of the Business" section.

Advertising Strategy
Your advertising strategy should consist of at least 4 out of the below 6 advertising media:

- Website: a website is mandatory for your business. A website provides the first impression that many potential clients will have about your company. If you have an unprofessional website, your chances of receiving a quote request diminish. On the other hand, having a professional and informative website will add instant credibility to your company. Be sure to include pictures of your inflatables and a link to your e-mail address for questions or quote requests. Do not include prices because it is always better to discuss prices verbally. Discussing prices verbally will give you the opportunity to communicate your company strengths so you can persuade the client to choose your company over the competition.
- Search Engine Optimization: paying a company for search engine optimization will increase your website's exposure and can increase the number of hits to your website.
- Google AdWords: allows you to display your ads on Google and their advertising network. You can reach users searching on Google or browsing websites in their content network, which can deliver your message to a targeted audience. You only pay if people click your ads. The Google content network comprises hundreds of thousands of high-quality websites, news pages, and blogs that partner with Google to display targeted AdWords ads. When you choose to advertise on the content network, you can expand your marketing reach to targeted audiences, and potential clients, visiting the content network sites every day.

- Yellow Pages (online or print): although the printed yellow pages are not as popular as they once were, they still provide a means for potential clients who lack internet savvy to find your company. However, if you would like to post an advertisement in the yellow pages, we suggest you post the advertisement online and forego the traditional yellow pages book that is printed and delivered to homes.
- Direct Mailers
  - Direct Mailers to Schools: create a list of schools in your target market by searching the internet. Draft a letter to each school and introduce them to your services. Be sure to include a color brochure that has pictures of your equipment. If they are interested in a fun activity, they will call you and request more information. .
  - Direct Mailers to Party Planners: create a list of party planners in your target market by searching the internet and yellow pages. Draft a letter to each party planner and introduce them to your services. Be sure to include a color brochure that has pictures of your equipment. One week after you mail your promotional material, call the party planner and ask if they have any questions. Explain your commission structure and give them an introduction to your company. Make a good first impression and do not be pushy. If you pressure the party planner, you will likely never hear back from them again.
  - Direct Mailers to Hotel Sales/Catering Managers: search the websites of all major hotel brands and create a list of hotels in your target market. Draft a letter to each sales/catering manager and introduce them to your services. Be sure to include a color brochure that has pictures of your equipment. One week after you mail your promotional material, call the sales/catering department of each hotel and ask if they have any questions. Explain your commission structure and give them an introduction to your company. Make a good first impression and do not be pushy. If you pressure the sales/catering manager, you will likely never hear

back from them again. If the hotel does not allow the sales/catering managers to receive a commission, then emphasize your high level of service and your quality equipment. If the sales/catering manager refers their client to your company and you do a great job, the client will be happy with the sales/catering manager and will continue to do business with that hotel. This is a win-win situation for both your company and the sales/catering manager.

- Business Cards and other Brochures: at each event, make sure you have business cards and brochures in a pouch that you tape to each inflatable. It is much easier for a guest to grab a card or brochure from the inflatable than to find you or the event manager for the night and ask him/her. All it takes is for the right person to take a $.05 business card and book a $1,000 party a few months later. This small investment can pay off big with word of mouth marketing.

Pricing

Pricing is a key component to the success of any business. If you price your services too high, you may lose a large segment of your market. If you price your services too low, you will attract clients who only care about price. You need to find a happy medium in your pricing strategy and build client loyalty. Client loyalty breeds word of mouth marketing. Word of mouth marketing is not only free, but it is also the most credible form of advertising. Once your company is established and word of mouth marketing spreads, you can spend less and less on traditional forms of advertising, thus increasing your profit margins.

In order to find out how much you should charge, you must find out how much your competition is charging. Refer to the "Market Analysis - Competition" section earlier for additional information.

If a client asks you to reduce your price, always have a lowest acceptable price you are willing to accept. If this lowest acceptable price does not satisfy your client, turn down the business. Explain to the client that they will receive the type of service they pay for and you cannot reduce your price any further.

Brand

By definition, a brand is a name, term, sign, symbol, design, or a combination of these, intended to identify the goods or services of one seller or group of sellers and to differentiate them from those of competitors. Branding will add value to your company because your clients view a brand as an important part of the service. Your brand is perhaps the greatest intangible asset your company will possess. Your brand is going to determine the long term success of your business. If your brand is weak, you will likely see shrinking profit margins that will eventually crush your business. If your brand is built on value, great service, and high quality equipment, then you will see long term growth and business expansion.

Database Marketing

Client satisfaction is great, but client loyalty will make your business a long term success. With every new client you receive, be sure to obtain specific information that you can use for database marketing. This information can include the client's telephone number, e-mail address, home address, birth date, anniversary date, and other special occasion dates. You can then use this information to contact previous clients continually throughout the year. This will ensure your company stays fresh in their minds and will increase the likelihood that they will become loyal clients and spread the positive word of mouth. Always keep the database updated with current information.

Sales Strategy

You will have to learn how to sell your services to clients whether you like selling or not. Although you may be paralyzed by the thought that you will have to be a salesperson, the fact of the matter is that all entrepreneurs are salespeople. Selling is actually quite easy. All you really need to do is tell the client what sets your company apart from your competition. Always be honest in your dealings and keep the sales message positive. Do not promise anything you cannot fulfill, as this is a sure way to create bad word of mouth.

Sales Incentives and Promotions

Sales promotions can be a great way to drum up business during slow times of the year. Sales promotions should be short-term incentives to encourage the purchase of your service. Whereas advertising and personal selling offer reasons to buy your service, sales promotions offer reasons to buy now. However, the ultimate goal is to have clients pay full price for your services. Relying on clients who always demand discounted prices will cheapen your brand and will ultimately ruin your business. We suggest you use the following types of sales promotions that will not cheapen your brand, but will increase client loyalty:

- Cash Discount: 10% discount for parties held within one month of the client's birthday.
- Cash Donation: 10% donation (based on the total price of the party) to non-profit groups who book their event with you.
- Inflatable Donation: offer a free inflatable when the client books a party that has a predetermined price. For example, if the client books a party for $1,000 or more, you can provide an additional inflatable for no extra charge.

Public Relations
Public relations is the process of building good relations with the public (newspaper articles, TV news stories, etc.) by obtaining favorable publicity, building up a good image, and handling or heading off unfavorable rumors and stories.

A public relations campaign has its distinct advantages and disadvantages. The major advantage of public relations is that it provides free publicity for your company. However, since public relations exposure is free, you cannot control whether the exposure is favorable or unfavorable. Before any public relations campaign is implemented, you must first research how public relations will affect your company. Press releases should be made available to newspapers and television stations to promote your service. However, the more exposure you receive as a small company, the greater the threat of competition becomes as copy-cat entrepreneurs piggy back off your idea. It would be best to gain local exposure and brand recognition before you decide to pursue a public relations campaign. Since the barriers to entry are relatively low for this type of business, your strategy should be to artificially raise the barriers to entry by dominating market share and making it difficult for new competitors to capture market share from your company.

Networking

Networking is going to be vital to growing your business. Networking is inexpensive and credible. It gives you the opportunity to personally interact with potential clients and directly sell your service. Networking is an ongoing task because no matter where you are or who you are talking to, you can discuss your business. At minimum, use your closest network to start spreading positive word of mouth (i.e. family and friends). When your business is officially open, tell your family and friends about your business and what types of products and services you offer. Ask them to spread the word by telling their friends.

Another great networking tool is joining a referral association. There are plenty of referral associations to choose from. Use the internet to find local referral associations that you can join. A popular referral association is BNI (www.bni.com). Referral associations offer members the opportunity to share ideas, contacts, and business referrals. You are tasked with referring business to fellow members and they refer business to you. Since other members of your referral association are recommending your business, this type of indirect selling is highly credible. This is a proven strategy to growing your business.

Also, volunteering your services to fundraising events and participating in community activities will increase your networking opportunities.

Client Service

<u>Description of Client Service Activities</u>
Initially, you will be the only client service specialist. All calls will be routed to your cell phone or a dedicated land line. Unless you are running this business full time, it is best to use a cell phone as your main business phone. Using a cell phone allows you to conduct business anytime, anywhere in the world.

You must present a very professional appearance and provide the highest level of client service possible whenever you are speaking to clients. If the client calls with a question and receives your voicemail, be sure to call the client back that day. If the client e-mails you, reply to the e-mail within 4 hours. This commitment to client service will breed long term client loyalty and long term profits. Once revenues allow, you may decide to hire a part-time employee whose job responsibilities will include client service.

<u>Expected Outcomes of Achieving Excellence</u>
The highest level of client service is the only way to achieve long term growth and success. Your company cannot afford to have any unsatisfied clients, as bad word of mouth will eventually ruin your company. Also, if your clients remain happy, they will order from you in the future and provide positive word of mouth, thus lowering advertising expenditures in the future.

Implementation of Marketing Strategy

In-house Responsibilities
As with any startup, you will be responsible for implementing your marketing strategy. You will need to network heavily and use your network to spread positive word of mouth for your company. You will also need to create flyers or brochures that you can send out to schools, hotels, party planners, and any other group you wish to market towards. Be sure to constantly update your marketing strategy based on what you find is working and what is not working.

Outsourced Functions
Outsourced marketing should only be considered if revenue and cash flow allow. Outsourced marketing functions include hiring an advertising agency, hiring graphic designers to create your marketing literature, and hiring a public relations firm to represent your company. These types of outsourced marketing and advertising functions are typically used by companies who have revenues in excess of $5,000,000 per year.

Assessment of Marketing Effectiveness

You need to make an assessment of how effective your marketing strategy is every 6 months. Calculate the return on investment (ROI) for each form of advertising media and redirect your marketing budget to the other forms of media which are generating the highest ROI. If an advertising media generates a negative ROI (meaning the cost of the media exceeds the profit the media generated), stop funding the media immediately.

Financial Documents

Financial Needs – Startup Expenses
You will need a budget of $10,000 to start a bounce house rental company. The funds can be in the form of cash, credit cards, or loans. The budget should be divided as follows:
- Equipment: $4,000: you will need enough equipment to buy any combination of the following equipment:
  - Standard bounce houses
  - Themed jumpers
  - Combo jumpers
  - Slide jumpers
  - Velcro wall jumpers
  - Bungee runs
  - Sumo suits
  - Party Extras (can include folding tables (length of tables vary from 4' to 10'), folding chairs, popcorn popping machines, table tennis tables, cotton candy machines, snow cone machines, etc.)
- Truck and/or Trailer: if you already have a pickup truck, then you do not need to buy a box truck or trailer during the early stages of your company. Only buy a box truck or trailer when you have a lot of equipment that needs to be mobile and housed in a secure location. If you already have a pickup truck and decide you need additional capacity, you can purchase a utility trailer for $4,000. If not, then use the $4,000 as a down payment for a box truck and finance the remaining balance.
- Insurance: $1,000 to $1,500: you will need both general liability insurance (for $1,000,000) and general property insurance (to cover your truck, trailer, and equipment). Refer to the "Insurance" section for additional information.
- Marketing: $500 to $1,000: refer to the "Marketing Strategy" section. Be sure to allocate your funds appropriately to maximize your return on investment.

Loan Dispersal Statement (needed only if seeking financing)
Based on your cash on hand, you can disperse your loan or credit card funds as you see fit according to your startup budget. It is important

not to grow too rapidly and outstrip your financing. Since the loan process can be tedious, you should really consider funding the business with credit cards if you do not have cash on hand. Once you start receiving positive cash flow, use 50% of the cash to fund growth and 50% of the cash to pay down your credit card debt. If you leverage your business too heavily with debt, you may never recover.

Credit Policy

Extending credit is not customary for a bounce house rental company. When you book an event, require a deposit to hold the date and collect the remaining balance the day of the event. Avoiding the headaches of accounts receivable will allow you to focus your time and energy on growing the business instead of collecting outstanding payments.

Business Bank Account

Some business owners open a separate business account with a bank to keep their personal and business expenses separate. This allows you to easily track income and expenses which enables you to evaluate your business' performance. If you would like to open up an account under the name of your business, you will need the following documents:

- Fictitious Business Name (DBA): if your business name is different from your personal name, you will be required to have a registered fictitious business name. You can file this at your county's Recorder Department for $20 to $80 per fictitious business name. To complete the registration process, you must announce your DBA to the public. This alerts the public that you are doing business under your DBA and not your personal name. Your county Recorder Department will have a list of local publications that will allow you to purchase an ad for several weeks so you can announce your DBA to the public. These ads typically cost less than $50.
- Employer Identification Number (EIN) (for partnerships and corporations only): you will need an EIN to provide to the bank. Obtaining an EIN is fast, easy, and free. Visit the IRS website at www.irs.gov and apply online. If your business is a sole proprietorship, all you need is your Social Security number.

- Partnership Agreement (partnerships only): the bank will need a copy of your partnership agreement. Make sure the partnership agreement is signed by all partners. Refer to the sample partnership agreement on the template page of the UBCG website.
- LLC Operating Agreement (LLC only): the bank will need a copy of your LLC operating agreement. Refer to the sample LLC operating agreement on the template page of the UBCG website.
- Articles of Incorporation (S-Corporations and C-Corporations only): the bank will need a copy of your articles of incorporation. Refer to the sample articles of incorporation on the template page of the UBCG website.

Break-even Analysis

The break-even point is the point at which a company's expenses exactly match the sales or service volume. It can be expressed in the following two ways:
- Total dollars or revenue exactly offset by total expenses, or
- Total units of production (cost of which exactly equals the income derived by their sales)

Since you are in the service industry, you will determine your breakeven point using the first calculation. This analysis can be done either mathematically or graphically. Revenue and expense figures are drawn from the income projections (refer to the "Three Year Income Statement Projection" section for income projections).

Tax Considerations

The type of business you operate determines the taxes you must pay and how you will pay them. There are four general kinds of business taxes.

Income Tax
Every business must file an annual income tax return. The form you use depends on the legal structure of your business. Income from your business is not subject to withholding. You typically pay the tax during the year as you earn your income. Sole proprietors, partners, or shareholders of an S-Corporation pay as they go by making regular tax payments based on the estimated annual tax for the year. If your independent contractors earn $600 or more in any given calendar year, you are also required to report their income to the IRS. It is the responsibility of the independent contractor to pay the required income taxes. Below is a breakdown detailing the various legal structures and what tax form you will need to file.

Legal Structure	IRS Form
Sole Proprietorship	Schedule C (Form 1040)
Partnership	Form 1065
Limited Liability Company	Schedule C (Form 1040)
S-Corporation	Form 1120S
C-Corporation	Form 1120 or 1120A

Forms and instructions for various types of business filings can be obtained for free at the Internal Revenue Service website (www.irs.gov).

Self-employment Tax
The self-employment tax is the Social Security tax for individuals who work for themselves, including sole proprietors and members of a partnership. The self-employment tax is figured and reported on Schedule SE, which is attached to and filed with Form 1040.

Employment Tax

If you have employees, you will probably be required to pay federal income tax withholding, Social Security and Medicare taxes, federal unemployment tax (Form 940 or Form 940EZ), and state income tax withholding.

Excise Tax

You may have to pay excise tax if you manufacture or sell certain products. Be sure to check with the federal, state, and local governments to identify excise taxes, permits, and licenses that may be required for your business.

Business License

A business license is a permit to sell a specific product or service in certain areas designated by state and local governments. Be sure to check with your city, county, and state governments regarding appropriate licensing requirements. Small business information can be obtained on most government websites or from the Small Business Administration website (www.sba.gov/hotlist/license.html).

Outsourced Tax Functions

Outsourced tax functions can include taking your tax return to a professional Certified Public Accountant (CPA) to complete the filing. Unless you are a CPA, we suggest you take your annual income statement and a list of all valid business deductions to your CPA or tax preparer at the end of each year. This will ensure all income is appropriately reported.

Three Year Income Statement Projection

The income statement shows your business' financial activity (revenues and expenses) over a period of time, usually monthly and/or annually. It is a moving picture showing what has happened in your business and is an excellent tool for assessing your business' health. Once your ledger is closed, the net income or loss is transferred to the balance sheet in the owner's equity section. Note that most accounting software programs can calculate common financial statements for you after all the appropriate information is recorded. The following 3 pages provide sample income statement projections that will look similar to the income statement projections you will prepare when writing your business plan.

Upstart Business Consulting Group
www.upstartbcg.com
Income Statement - Year 1

	January Month 1	February Month 2	March Month 3	April Month 4	May Month 5	June Month 6	July Month 7	August Month 8	September Month 9	October Month 10	November Month 11	December Month 12	Year-to-date Total
Revenue													
Sales Revenue	$ 810	$ 2,955	$ 868	$ 1,960	$ 663	$ 875	$ 200	$ 4,200	$ 2,916	$ 1,140	$ 445	$ 3,887	$ 20,918
Other Sales (Advertising, etc.)	-	-	-	-	-	-	-	-	-	-	-	-	-
Total Revenue	810	2,955	868	1,960	663	875	200	4,200	2,916	1,140	445	3,887	20,918
Cost of Good Sold													
Direct Labor	243	887	260	588	199	263	60	1,260	875	342	134	1,166	6,276
Materials	20	20	20	20	20	20	20	20	20	20	20	20	240
Total Cost of Goods Sold	263	907	280	608	219	283	80	1,280	895	362	154	1,186	6,516
Gross Margin	547	2,049	588	1,352	444	593	120	2,920	2,021	778	292	2,701	14,403
Selling, General, Admin. Exp.													
Sales and Marketing	242	47	25	25	25	25	25	25	25	25	25	25	539
General & Administrative	128	95	95	95	95	95	95	95	95	95	95	95	1,175
Depreciation	122	122	122	122	122	122	122	122	122	122	122	122	1,467
Total SGA Expenses	491	264	242	242	242	242	242	242	242	242	242	242	3,180
Operating Income (Loss)	55	1,784	345	1,110	202	350	(122)	2,678	1,779	536	49	2,458	11,223
Interest Expense (Income)	-	-	-	-	-	-	-	-	-	-	-	-	-
Income (Loss) Before Taxes	55	1,784	345	1,110	202	350	(122)	2,678	1,779	536	49	2,458	11,223
Income Tax (Credit)	19	607	117	377	69	119	(42)	910	605	182	17	836	3,816
Income (Loss) After Taxes	$ 37	$ 1,177	$ 228	$ 732	$ 133	$ 231	$ (81)	$ 1,767	$ 1,174	$ 353	$ 32	$ 1,623	$ 7,407
Less: Distributions	-	-	-	-	-	-	-	-	-	-	-	-	-
Remaining Net Income	$ 37	$ 1,177	$ 228	$ 732	$ 133	$ 231	$ (81)	$ 1,767	$ 1,174	$ 353	$ 32	$ 1,623	$ 7,407

Upstart Business Consulting Group

www.upstartbcg.com

Income Statement - Year 2

	January Month 1	February Month 2	March Month 3	April Month 4	May Month 5	June Month 6	July Month 7	August Month 8	September Month 9	October Month 10	November Month 11	December Month 12	Year-to-date Total
Revenue													
Sales Revenue	$1,215	$4,433	$1,302	$2,940	$995	$1,313	$300	$6,300	$4,374	$1,710	$668	$5,831	$31,378
Other Sales (Advertising, etc.)	-	-	-	-	-	-	-	-	-	-	-	-	-
Total Revenue	1,215	4,433	1,302	2,940	995	1,313	300	6,300	4,374	1,710	668	5,831	31,378
Cost of Good Sold													
Direct Labor	364	1,330	391	882	298	394	90	1,890	1,312	513	200	1,749	9,413
Materials	30	75	75	75	75	75	-	75	75	75	75	75	780
Total Cost of Goods Sold	394	1,405	466	957	373	469	90	1,965	1,387	588	275	1,824	10,193
Gross Margin	820	3,028	836	1,983	621	844	210	4,335	2,987	1,122	392	4,006	21,184
Selling, General, Admin. Exp.													
Sales and Marketing	25	25	25	25	25	25	25	25	25	25	25	25	300
General & Administrative	95	95	95	95	95	95	95	95	95	95	95	95	1,143
Depreciation	122	122	122	122	122	122	122	122	122	122	122	122	1,467
Total SGA Expenses	242	242	242	242	242	242	242	242	242	242	242	242	2,909
Operating Income (Loss)	578	2,785	594	1,741	379	601	(32)	4,093	2,744	880	150	3,764	18,275
Interest Expense (Income)	-	-	-	-	-	-	-	-	-	-	-	-	-
Income (Loss) Before Taxes	578	2,785	594	1,741	379	601	(32)	4,093	2,744	880	150	3,764	18,275
Income Tax (Credit)	196	947	202	592	129	204	(11)	1,391	933	299	51	1,280	6,214
Income (Loss) After Taxes	$381	$1,838	$392	$1,149	$250	$397	$(21)	$2,701	$1,811	$581	$99	$2,484	12,062
Less: Distributions	-	-	-	-	-	-	-	-	-	-	-	-	-
Remaining Net Income	$381	$1,838	$392	$1,149	$250	$397	$(21)	$2,701	$1,811	$581	$99	$2,484	$12,062

Upstart Business Consulting Group

www.upstartbcg.com

Income Statement - Year 3

	January	February	March	April	May	June	July	August	September	October	November	December	Year-to-date
	Month 1	Month 2	Month 3	Month 4	Month 5	Month 6	Month 7	Month 8	Month 9	Month 10	Month 11	Month 12	Total
Revenue													
Sales Revenue	$1,822	$6,649	$1,953	$4,410	$1,492	$1,969	$450	$9,450	$6,560	$2,565	$1,001	$8,746	$47,066
Other Sales (Advertising, etc.)	-	-	-	-	-	-	-	-	-	-	-	-	-
Total Revenue	1,822	6,649	1,953	4,410	1,492	1,969	450	9,450	6,560	2,565	1,001	8,746	47,066
Cost of Good Sold													
Direct Labor	547	1,995	586	1,323	448	591	135	2,835	1,968	770	300	2,624	14,120
Materials	30	75	75	75	75	75	-	75	75	75	75	75	780
Total Cost of Goods Sold	577	2,070	661	1,398	523	666	135	2,910	2,043	845	375	2,699	14,900
Gross Margin	1,245	4,579	1,292	3,012	969	1,303	315	6,540	4,517	1,721	626	6,047	32,166
Selling, General, Admin. Exp.													
Sales and Marketing	25	25	25	25	25	25	25	25	25	25	25	25	300
General & Administrative	95	95	95	95	95	95	95	95	95	95	95	95	1,143
Depreciation	122	122	122	122	122	122	122	122	122	122	122	122	1,467
Total SGA Expenses	242	242	242	242	242	242	242	242	242	242	242	242	2,909
Operating Income (Loss)	1,003	4,337	1,050	2,770	727	1,061	73	6,298	4,275	1,478	383	5,805	29,257
Interest Expense (Income)	-	-	-	-	-	-	-	-	-	-	-	-	-
Income (Loss) Before Taxes	1,003	4,337	1,050	2,770	727	1,061	73	6,298	4,275	1,478	383	5,805	29,257
Income Tax (Credit)	341	1,474	357	942	247	361	25	2,141	1,453	503	130	1,974	9,947
Income (Loss) After Taxes	$662	$2,862	$693	$1,828	$480	$700	$48	$4,156	$2,821	$976	$253	$3,831	$19,310
Less: Distributions	-	-	-	-	-	-	-	-	-	-	-	-	-
Remaining Net Income	$662	$2,862	$693	$1,828	$480	$700	$48	$4,156	$2,821	$976	$253	$3,831	$19,310

Three Year Balance Sheet Projection

The balance sheet shows your business' financial position (assets, liabilities, and owner's equity) over a period of time, usually monthly and/or annually. It is a moving picture showing what has happened in your business and is an excellent tool for assessing your business' health. Once your ledger is closed and balanced, the revenue and expense totals are transferred to this statement. The following 3 pages provide sample balance sheet statement projections that will look similar to the balance sheet statement projections you will prepare when writing your business plan.

Upstart Business Consulting Group
www.upstarfbcg.com
Balance Sheet - Year 1

	January Month 1	February Month 2	March Month 3	April Month 4	May Month 5	June Month 6	July Month 7	August Month 8	September Month 9	October Month 10	November Month 11	December Month 12
Assets												
Current Assets												
Cash & Cash Equivalents	$ 3,159	$ 4,458	$ 4,208	$ 5,063	$ 5,318	$ 5,707	$ 5,748	$ 7,637	$ 8,934	$ 9,409	$ 9,564	$ 11,309
Accounts Receivable	-	-	600	600	600	600	600	600	600	600	600	600
Inventory												
Other Current Assets												
Total Current Assets	3,159	4,458	4,808	5,663	5,918	6,307	6,348	8,237	9,534	10,009	10,164	11,909
Property & Equipment												
General Equipment	4,000	4,000	4,000	4,000	4,000	4,000	4,000	4,000	4,000	4,000	4,000	4,000
Automobile	4,000	4,000	4,000	4,000	4,000	4,000	4,000	4,000	4,000	4,000	4,000	4,000
Computer	800	800	800	800	800	800	800	800	800	800	800	800
Less: Accumulated Depreciation	(122)	(244)	(367)	(489)	(611)	(733)	(856)	(978)	(1,100)	(1,222)	(1,344)	(1,467)
Net Property & Equipment	8,678	8,556	8,433	8,311	8,189	8,067	7,944	7,822	7,700	7,578	7,456	7,333
Other Long-Term Assets												
Total Long-Term Assets	8,678	8,556	8,433	8,311	8,189	8,067	7,944	7,822	7,700	7,578	7,456	7,333
Total Assets	$ 11,837	$ 13,014	$ 13,242	$ 13,974	$ 14,107	$ 14,373	$ 14,292	$ 16,060	$ 17,234	$ 17,587	$ 17,619	$ 19,242
Liabilities & Equity												
Current Liabilities												
Accounts Payable	$ 1,000	$ 1,000	$ 1,000	$ 1,000	$ 1,000	$ 1,000	$ 1,000	$ 1,000	$ 1,000	$ 1,000	$ 1,000	$ 1,000
Short-Term Borrowing												
Other Current Liabilities												
Total Current Liabilities	1,000	1,000	1,000	1,000	1,000	1,000	1,000	1,000	1,000	1,000	1,000	1,000
Long Term Debt												
Other Long-Term Liabilities												
Total Long-Term Liabilities												
Total Liabilities	1,000	1,000	1,000	1,000	1,000	1,000	1,000	1,000	1,000	1,000	1,000	1,000
Owners Equity												
Owner's Investment (Contribution)	10,800	10,800	10,800	10,800	10,800	10,800	10,800	10,800	10,800	10,800	10,800	10,800
Retained Earnings - Prior Period	-	37	1,214	1,442	2,174	2,307	2,538	2,457	4,225	5,399	5,752	5,784
Retained Earnings - Current Period	37	1,177	228	732	133	231	(81)	1,767	1,174	353	32	1,623
Total Owners Equity	10,837	12,014	12,242	12,974	13,107	13,338	13,257	15,025	16,199	16,552	16,584	18,207
Total Liabilities & Equity	$ 11,837	$ 13,014	$ 13,242	$ 13,974	$ 14,107	$ 14,338	$ 14,257	$ 16,025	$ 17,199	$ 17,552	$ 17,584	$ 19,207

Upstart Business Consulting Group
www.upstartbcg.com
Balance Sheet - Year 2

	January Month 1	February Month 2	March Month 3	April Month 4	May Month 5	June Month 6	July Month 7	August Month 8	September Month 9	October Month 10	November Month 11	December Month 12
Assets												
Current Assets												
Cash & Cash Equivalents	$ 10,412	$ 10,914	$12,078	$12,595	$ 14,212	$ 15,403	$ 14,962	$ 16,396	$ 14,033	$ 15,260	$ 16,327	$ 15,327
Accounts Receivable	2,000	1,000	600	500	2,000	1,000	1,500	1,000	4,000	3,000	2,000	3,000
Inventory	-	-	-	-	-	-	-	-	-	-	-	-
Other Current Assets	-	-	-	-	-	-	-	-	-	-	-	-
Total Current Assets	12,412	11,914	12,678	13,095	16,212	16,403	16,462	17,396	18,033	18,260	18,327	18,327
Property & Equipment												
General Equipment	4,000	4,000	4,000	4,000	4,000	4,000	4,000	4,000	4,000	4,000	4,000	4,000
Automobile	4,000	4,000	4,000	4,000	4,000	4,000	4,000	4,000	4,000	4,000	4,000	4,000
Computer	800	800	800	800	800	800	800	800	800	800	800	800
Less: Accumulated Depreciation	(1,589)	(1,711)	(1,833)	(1,956)	(2,078)	(2,200)	(2,322)	(2,444)	(2,567)	(2,689)	(2,811)	(2,933)
Net Property & Equipment	7,211	7,089	6,967	6,844	6,722	6,600	6,478	6,356	6,233	6,111	5,989	5,867
Other Long-Term Assets	-	-	-	-	-	-	-	-	-	-	-	-
Total Long-Term Assets	7,211	7,089	6,967	6,844	6,722	6,600	6,478	6,356	6,233	6,111	5,989	5,867
Total Assets	$19,623	$19,003	$19,645	$19,939	$22,934	$23,003	$22,940	$23,752	$24,267	$24,371	$24,316	$24,193
Liabilities & Equity												
Current Liabilities												
Accounts Payable	$ 1,000	$ 1,000	$ 1,000	$ 1,000	$ 1,000	$ 1,000	$ 1,000	$ 1,000	$ 1,000	$ 1,000	$ 1,000	$ 1,000
Short-Term Borrowing	-	-	-	-	-	-	-	-	-	-	-	-
Other Current Liabilities	-	-	-	-	-	-	-	-	-	-	-	-
Total Current Liabilities	1,000	1,000	1,000	1,000	1,000	1,000	1,000	1,000	1,000	1,000	1,000	1,000
Long Term Debt	-	-	-	-	-	-	-	-	-	-	-	-
Other Long-Term Liabilities	-	-	-	-	-	-	-	-	-	-	-	-
Total Long-Term Liabilities	-	-	-	-	-	-	-	-	-	-	-	-
Total Liabilities	1,000	1,000	1,000	1,000	1,000	1,000	1,000	1,000	1,000	1,000	1,000	1,000
Owners Equity												
Owner's Investment (Contribution)	10,800	8,342	8,592	7,737	10,482	10,093	10,052	8,163	6,866	6,391	6,236	4,491
Retained Earnings - Prior Period	7,407	7,788	9,627	10,019	11,167	11,417	11,814	11,793	14,494	16,305	16,885	16,984
Retained Earnings - Current Period	381	1,838	392	1,149	250	397	(21)	2,701	1,811	581	99	1,623
Total Owners Equity	18,588	17,968	18,610	18,904	21,899	21,908	21,845	22,656	23,171	23,276	23,221	23,098
Total Liabilities & Equity	$19,588	$18,968	$19,610	$19,904	$22,899	$22,908	$22,845	$23,656	$24,171	$24,276	$24,221	$24,098

Upstart Business Consulting Group
www.upstartbcg.com
Balance Sheet - Year 3

	January	February	March	April	May	June	July	August	September	October	November	December
	Month 1	Month 2	Month 3	Month 4	Month 5	Month 6	Month 7	Month 8	Month 9	Month 10	Month 11	Month12
Assets												
Current Assets												
Cash & Cash Equivalents	$ 18,702	$ 19,702	$ 20,702	$ 20,802	$ 22,302	$ 23,302	$ 22,802	$ 23,302	$ 20,302	$ 21,302	$ 22,302	$ 21,302
Accounts Receivable	2,000	1,000	600	500	2,000	1,000	1,500	1,000	4,000	3,000	2,000	3,000
Inventory	-	-	-	-	-	-	-	-	-	-	-	-
Other Current Assets	-	-	-	-	-	-	-	-	-	-	-	-
Total Current Assets	20,702	20,702	21,302	21,302	24,302	24,302	24,302	24,302	24,302	24,302	24,302	24,302
Property & Equipment												
General Equipment	4,000	4,000	4,000	4,000	4,000	4,000	4,000	4,000	4,000	4,000	4,000	4,000
Automobile	4,000	4,000	4,000	4,000	4,000	4,000	4,000	4,000	4,000	4,000	4,000	4,000
Computer	800	800	800	800	800	800	800	800	800	800	800	800
Less: Accumulated Depreciation	(122)	(244)	(367)	(489)	(611)	(733)	(856)	(978)	(1,100)	(1,222)	(1,344)	(1,467)
Net Property & Equipment	8,678	8,556	8,433	8,311	8,189	8,067	7,944	7,822	7,700	7,578	7,456	7,333
Other Long-Term Assets	-	-	-	-	-	-	-	-	-	-	-	-
Total Long-Term Assets	8,678	8,556	8,433	8,311	8,189	8,067	7,944	7,822	7,700	7,578	7,456	7,333
Total Assets	$ 29,380	$ 29,258	$ 29,735	$ 29,613	$ 32,491	$ 32,369	$ 32,247	$ 32,124	$ 32,002	$ 31,880	$ 31,758	$ 31,635
Liabilities & Equity												
Current Liabilities												
Accounts Payable	$ 1,000	$ 1,000	$ 1,000	$ 1,000	$ 1,000	$ 1,000	$ 1,000	$ 1,000	$ 1,000	$ 1,000	$ 1,000	$ 1,000
Short-Term Borrowing	-	-	-	-	-	-	-	-	-	-	-	-
Other Current Liabilities	-	-	-	-	-	-	-	-	-	-	-	-
Total Current Liabilities	1,000	1,000	1,000	1,000	1,000	1,000	1,000	1,000	1,000	1,000	1,000	1,000
Long Term Debt	-	-	-	-	-	-	-	-	-	-	-	-
Other Long-Term Liabilities	-	-	-	-	-	-	-	-	-	-	-	-
Total Long-Term Liabilities												
Total Liabilities	1,000	1,000	1,000	1,000	1,000	1,000	1,000	1,000	1,000	1,000	1,000	1,000
Owners Equity												
Owner's Investment (Contribution)	9,641	8,342	8,592	7,737	10,482	10,093	10,052	8,163	6,866	6,391	6,236	4,491
Retained Earnings - Prior Period	18,607	18,643	19,821	20,049	20,781	20,914	21,145	21,064	22,832	24,005	24,359	24,391
Retained Earnings - Current Period	37	1,177	228	732	133	231	(81)	1,767	1,174	353	32	1,623
Total Owners Equity	28,285	28,163	28,640	28,518	31,396	31,239	31,116	30,994	30,872	30,750	30,628	30,505
Total Liabilities & Equity	$ 29,285	$ 29,163	$ 29,640	$ 29,518	$ 32,396	$ 32,239	$ 32,116	$ 31,994	$ 31,872	$ 31,750	$ 31,628	$ 31,505

78

Three Year Cash Flow Projection

The cash flow statement projects what your business plan means in terms of dollars. It shows cash inflow and outflow over a period of time (usually monthly and/or annually) and is used for internal planning. If you are taking out a loan to fund your business, it is of prime interest to the lender and shows how you intend to repay your loan. Cash flow statements show both how much and when cash must flow in and out of your business. The following 3 pages provide sample cash flow statement projections that will look similar to the cash flow statement projections you will prepare when writing your business plan.

Upstart Business Consulting Group

www.upstartbcg.com

Cash Flow - Year 1

	January Month 1	February Month 2	March Month 3	April Month 4	May Month 5	June Month 6	July Month 7	August Month 8	September Month 9	October Month 10	November Month 11	December Month 12
Cash flows from operating activities:												
Net Income	$ 55	$ 1,784	$ 345	$1,110	$ 202	$ 350	$ (122)	$2,678	$ 1,779	$ 536	$ 49	$ 2,458
Adjustments to reconcile net income to net cash provided by operating activities (change in):												
Depreciation	122	122	122	122	122	122	122	122	122	122	122	122
Accounts Receivable	-	-	(600)	-	-	-	-	-	-	-	-	-
Other current assets	-	-	-	-	-	-	-	-	-	-	-	-
Accounts Payable	1,000	-	-	-	-	-	-	-	-	-	-	-
Other current liabilities	-	-	-	-	-	-	-	-	-	-	-	-
Other net cash inflows (outflows)	(19)	(607)	(118)	(377)	(68)	(84)	41	(910)	(604)	(183)	(16)	(836)
Net cash provided by (used in) operating activities	1,159	1,300	(251)	855	256	388	41	1,890	1,297	475	155	1,745
Cash flows from investing activities:												
Sale (Purchase) of Equipment	(8,800)	-	-	-	-	-	-	-	-	-	-	-
Net cash provided by (used in) investing activities	(8,800)	-	-	-	-	-	-	-	-	-	-	-
Cash flows from financing activities:												
Proceeds (payments) of short-term debt, net	-	-	-	-	-	-	-	-	-	-	-	-
Proceeds (payments) of long-term debt, net	-	-	-	-	-	-	-	-	-	-	-	-
Contributions (owner equity)	10,800	-	-	-	-	-	-	-	-	-	-	-
Distributions to owners & shareholders	-	-	-	-	-	-	-	-	-	-	-	-
Net cash provided by (used in) financing activities	10,800	-	-	-	-	-	-	-	-	-	-	-
Net increase (decrease) in cash and cash equivalents	3,159	1,300	(251)	855	256	388	41	1,890	1,297	475	155	1,745
Cash and cash equivalents at beginning of period	-	3,159	4,458	4,208	5,063	5,318	5,707	5,748	7,637	8,934	9,409	9,564
Cash and cash equivalents at end of period	$3,159	$4,458	$4,208	$5,063	$5,318	$5,707	$5,748	$7,637	$8,934	$9,409	$9,564	$11,309

80

Upstart Business Consulting Group

www.upstartbcg.com

Cash Flow – Year 2

	January Month 1	February Month 2	March Month 3	April Month 4	May Month 5	June Month 6	July Month 7	August Month 8	September Month 9	October Month 10	November Month 11	December Month 12
Cash flows from operating activities:												
Net Income	$ 1,215	$ 4,433	$ 1,302	$ 2,940	$ 995	$ 1,313	$ 300	$ 6,300	$ 4,374	$ 1,710	$ 668	$ 5,831
Adjustments to reconcile net income to net cash provided by operating activities (change in):												
Depreciation	122	122	122	122	122	122	122	122	122	122	122	122
Accounts Receivable	1,400	(1,000)	(400)	(100)	1,500	(1,000)	500	(500)	3,000	(1,000)	(1,000)	1,000
Other current assets	-	-	-	-	-	-	-	-	-	-	-	-
Accounts Payable	-	-	-	-	-	-	-	-	-	-	-	-
Other current liabilities												
Other net cash inflows (outflows)	(3,633)	(595)	(110)	(1,591)	(3,744)	1,145	(1,322)	(2,599)	(8,563)	871	1,432	(6,208)
Net cash provided by (used in) operating activities	(896)	2,960	914	1,371	(1,127)	1,580	(399)	3,323	(1,067)	1,703	1,222	745
Cash flows from investing activities:												
Sale (Purchase) of Equipment	-	-	-	-	-	-	-	-	-	-	-	-
Net cash provided by (used in) investing activities	-	-	-	-	-	-	-	-	-	-	-	-
Cash flows from financing activities:												
Proceeds (payments) of short-term debt, net	-	-	-	-	-	-	-	-	-	-	-	-
Proceeds (payments) of long-term debt, net	-	-	-	-	-	-	-	-	-	-	-	-
Contributions (owner equity)	-	(2,458)	250	(855)	2,745	(388)	(41)	(1,889)	(1,296)	(476)	(155)	(1,745)
Distributions to owners & shareholders	-	-	-	-	-	-	-	-	-	-	-	-
Net cash provided by (used in) financing activities	-	(2,458)	250	(855)	2,745	(388)	(41)	(1,889)	(1,296)	(476)	(155)	(1,745)
Net increase (decrease) in cash and cash equivalents	(896)	501	1,164	517	1,617	1,191	(441)	1,434	(2,363)	1,228	1,067	(1,000)
Cash and cash equivalents at beginning of period	11,309	10,412	10,914	12,078	12,595	14,212	15,403	14,963	16,396	14,033	15,261	16,328
Cash and cash equivalents at end of period	$10,412	$10,914	$12,078	$12,595	$14,212	$15,403	$14,963	$16,396	$14,033	$15,261	$16,328	$15,328

Upstart Business Consulting Group

www.upstartbcg.com

Cash Flow - Year 3

	January Month 1	February Month 2	March Month 3	April Month 4	May Month 5	June Month 6	July Month 7	August Month 8	September Month 9	October Month 10	November Month 11	December Month 12
Cash flows from operating activities:												
Net Income	$ 1,822	$ 6,649	$ 1,953	$ 4,410	$ 1,492	$ 1,969	$ 450	$ 9,450	$ 6,560	$ 2,565	$ 1,001	$ 8,746
Adjustments to reconcile net income to net cash provided by operating activities (change in):												
Depreciation	122	122	122	122	122	122	122	122	122	122	122	122
Accounts Receivable	(1,000)	(1,000)	(400)	(100)	1,500	(1,000)	500	(500)	3,000	(1,000)	(1,000)	1,000
Other current assets	-	-	-	-	-	-	-	-	-	-	-	-
Accounts Payable	-	-	-	-	-	-	-	-	-	-	-	-
Other current liabilities	-	-	-	-	-	-	-	-	-	-	-	-
Other net cash inflows (outflows)	(2,719)	(3,471)	(925)	(3,478)	(4,358)	297	(1,531)	(6,683)	(11,386)	(212)	1,031	(9,123)
Net cash provided by (used in) operating activities	(1,775)	2,300	750	954	(1,244)	1,388	(459)	2,389	(1,703)	1,475	1,154	745
Cash flows from investing activities:												
Sale (Purchase) of Equipment	-	-	-	-	-	-	-	-	-	-	-	-
Net cash provided by (used in) investing activities	-	-	-	-	-	-	-	-	-	-	-	-
Cash flows from financing activities:												
Proceeds (payments) of short-term debt, net	-	-	-	-	-	-	-	-	-	-	-	-
Proceeds (payments) of long-term debt, net	-	-	-	-	-	-	-	-	-	-	-	-
Contributions (owner equity)	5,150	(1,300)	250	(855)	2,745	(388)	(41)	(1,889)	(1,296)	(476)	(155)	(1,745)
Distributions to owners & shareholders	-	-	-	-	-	-	-	-	-	-	-	-
Net cash provided by (used in) financing activities	5,150	(1,300)	250	(855)	2,745	(388)	(41)	(1,889)	(1,296)	(476)	(155)	(1,745)
Net increase (decrease) in cash and cash equivalents	3,375	1,000	1,000	100	1,501	1,000	(500)	500	(2,999)	1,000	1,000	(1,000)
Cash and cash equivalents at beginning of period	15,327	18,702	19,702	20,702	20,802	22,302	23,302	22,802	23,302	20,302	21,302	22,302
Cash and cash equivalents at end of period	$18,702	$19,702	$20,702	$20,802	$22,302	$23,302	$22,802	$23,302	$20,302	$21,302	$22,302	$21,302

Additional Forecasting Charts

	January	February	March	April	May	June	July	August	September	October	November	December	Total
	Month 1	Month 2	Month 3	Month 4	Month 5	Month 6	Month 7	Month 8	Month 9	Month 10	Month 11	Month12	
Year 1	810	2,955	868	1,960	663	875	200	4,200	2,916	1,140	445	3,887	20,918
Year 2	1,215	4,433	1,302	2,940	995	1,313	300	6,300	4,374	1,710	668	5,831	31,378
Year 3	1,822	6,649	1,953	4,410	1,492	1,969	450	9,450	6,560	2,565	1,001	8,746	47,066

Revenue Seasonality

— Year 1   — Year 2   — Year 3

Seasonality Trends

Depending on your type of business, you will encounter seasonal trends where sales will either increase or decrease. It is helpful to chart your sales so you can observe the seasonality trends of your specific business, which will help you make proper marketing decisions.

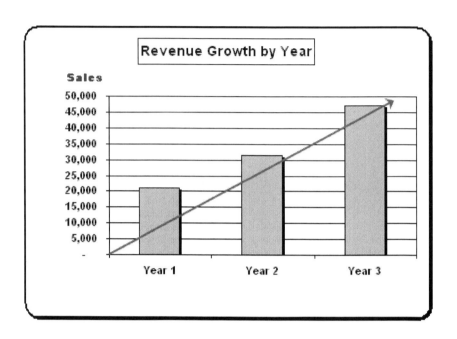

Revenue Growth by Year

* Note that it is not unusual to experience 40% to 50% growth in your first few years of business when you are highly motivated, sufficiently market your products and/ or services, and continually build your customer base.

Supporting Documents

This section of your business plan will contain all of the records that back up the statements and decisions made in the main sections of your business plan. The most common supporting documents include:

Personal Resumes
Include resumes for owners and management. A resume should be a one-page document and include the following information:
- Work history
- Educational background
- Professional affiliations and honors
- Special skills relating to the company position

Refer to the sample personal resume on the template page of the UBCG website.

Owners Financial Statements
Include personal financial statements for each owner. The financial statement will show assets and liabilities held outside the business as well as personal net worth. Owners will often have to draw on personal assets to finance the business, and these statements will show what is available. Bankers and investors usually want this information as well. Refer to the sample personal financial statement on the template page of the UBCG website.

Credit Reports
You will need credit reports for each partner in the company. Credit reports can be received from any of the 3 major credit reporting agencies (Experian, Transunion, and Equifax). You can logon to www.annualcreditreport.com to access your credit reports from each of the 3 above credit reporting agencies once every 12 months. This service is free as required by federal law.

Copies of Leases, Mortgages, and other Agreements
All agreements currently in force between your company and a leasing agency, mortgage company, or other agency should be included here.

Letters of Reference
Letters recommending you as being a reputable and reliable business person worthy of being considered a good risk (both business and personal references). Letters of reference are particularly important when applying for a loan.

Contracts
Include all business contracts, both completed and currently in force.

Other Legal Documents
All legal papers pertaining to your legal structure, proprietary rights, insurance, shipping contracts, and all other legal documents.

Miscellaneous Documents
All other documents which have been referred to, but not included in the main body of the plan (e.g. location plans, demographics, competition analysis, advertising rate sheets, cost analysis, etc.).

Appendix A: Financial Ratios

Return on Investment (ROI)

$$ROI = \frac{(\text{Gain from Investment} - \text{Cost of Investment})}{\text{Cost of Investment}}$$

Return on Assets (ROA)

$$ROA = \frac{\text{Net Income}}{\text{Total Assets}}$$

Return on Equity (ROE)

$$ROE = \frac{\text{Net Income}}{\text{Average Shareholder Equity}}$$

Asset Turnover

$$\text{Asset Turnover} = \frac{\text{Sales}}{\text{Assets}}$$

Payback Period (in years)

$$\text{Payback Period} = \frac{\text{Initial Investment}}{\text{Annual Net Income}}$$

Appendix B: Helpful Websites

www.upstartbcg.com - Upstart Business Consulting Group home page

www.annualcreditreport.com - Resource for obtaining credit reports for potential partners

www.bni.com - A popular referral association for generating customers

www.investopedia.com - Summary of financial ratios and information

www.irs.gov - Internal Revenue Service, useful for federal tax forms and rules

www.quickbooks.com - A website where you can purchase accounting software

www.sba.gov - United States Small Business Administration (SBA)

www.sba.gov/hotlist/license.html - State business license information

www.score.org – Service Corp of Retired Executives (SCORE)

www.taxcut.com - Software for preparing tax forms yourself

www.turbotax.com - Software for preparing tax forms yourself

www.usa.gov/Agencies/State_and_Territories.shtml - State government local websites and information

www.womma.org - Word of Mouth Marketing Association

Appendix C: Business Template Instructions

In order to access the free list of business templates, please log on to the Upstart Business Consulting Group website (www.upstartbcg.com) and browse to the secured "Templates" page. In order to gain access to the free business templates, you must input the following credentials:

User ID: UBCG
Password: Upstart1

Once you are granted access to the secured "Templates" page, click on the business template you want to download. A pop-up window will prompt you to save the file to your computer. Click the "save" button and select the location on your computer where you want to save the file. You can then reference the file on your own computer without logging in to the Upstart Business Consulting Group website.

Appendix D: Glossary

The glossary contains various terms that you may want to use when drafting your business plan.

Advertising - Any paid form of non-personal presentation and promotion of ideas, goods, or services by an identified sponsor

Advertising agency - A marketing services firm that assists companies in planning, preparing, implementing, and evaluating all or portions of their advertising programs

Advertising objective - A specific communication task to be accomplished with a specific target audience during a specific period of time

Asset turnover - Measures the efficiency of a company's use of its assets in generating sales revenue or sales income to the company

Baby boom - The significant increase in the annual birthrate following World War II and lasting until the early 1960s. The "baby boomers," now moving into middle age, are a prime target for marketers

Belief - A descriptive thought that a person holds about something

Benchmarking - The process of comparing the company's products and processes to those of competitors or leading firms in other industries to find ways to improve quality and performance

Bootstrap financing - Starting a business without the assistance of outside investors or additional debt. Examples include personal credit cards and savings

Brand - A name, term, sign, symbol, or design, or a combination of these intended to identify the goods or services of one seller or group of sellers and to differentiate them from those of competitors

Brand equity - The value of a brand, based on the extent to which it has high brand loyalty, name awareness, perceived quality, strong brand associations, and other assets such as patents, trademarks, and channel relationships

Brand extension - Using a successful brand name to launch a new or modified product in a new category

Break-even - The point at which total sales equals total costs. Net income equals zero

Business analysis - A review of the sales, costs, and profit projections for a new product to find out whether these factors satisfy the company's objectives

Buyer - The third party that exchanges consideration (money) for the products being sold

Buyer-readiness stages - The stages consumers normally pass through on their way to purchase, including awareness, knowledge, liking, preference, conviction, and purchase

By-product pricing - Setting a price for by-products in order to make the main product's price more competitive

Captive-product pricing - Setting a price for products that must be used along with an artificially low-priced main product, such as blades for a razor and film for a camera

Cash discount - A price reduction offered by companies to buyers who pay their bills promptly

Competition-based pricing - Setting prices based on the prices that competitors charge for similar products

Competitive advantage - An advantage over competitors gained by offering consumers greater value, either through lower prices or by providing more benefits that justify higher prices

Competitive marketing strategies - Strategies that strongly position the company against competitors and that give the company the strongest possible strategic advantage

Competitor analysis - The process of identifying key competitors; assessing their objectives, strategies, strengths and weaknesses, and reaction patterns; and selecting which competitors to attack or avoid

Consumer buying behavior - The buying behavior of final consumers-individuals and households who buy goods and services for personal consumption

Contests, sweepstakes, games - Promotional events that give consumers the chance to win something by luck or through extra effort (e.g. cash, trips, or something else a consumer may value)

Core competency - An organization's major value creating skills, capabilities, and resources that determine its competitive weapons

Cost of goods sold - The net cost to the company of goods sold

Cost-plus pricing - Adding a standard markup to the cost of the product

Coupon - Certificate that gives buyers a saving when they purchase a specified product

Credibility - When customers perceive you as being honest and competent

Current ratio - Measure of the business' liquidity and how easily the company can pay current term debts

Customer lifetime value - The amount by which revenues from a given customer over time will exceed the company's costs of attracting, selling, and servicing that customer

Customer sales force structure - A sales force organization under which salespeople specialize in selling only to certain customers or industries

Customer satisfaction - The extent to which a product's perceived performance matches a buyer's expectations. If the product's performance falls short of expectations, the buyer is dissatisfied. If performance matches or exceeds expectations, the buyer is satisfied or delighted

Deciders - People in the organization's buying center who have formal or informal power to select or approve the final suppliers

Demand curve - A curve that shows the number of units the market will buy in a given time period at different prices that might be charged

Demands - Human wants that are backed by buying power

Demographic segmentation - Dividing the market into groups based on demographic variables such as age, gender, family size, family life cycle, income, occupation, education, religion, race, and nationality

Differentiated marketing - A market-coverage strategy in which a firm decides to target several market segments and designs separate offers for each

Direct marketing - Direct communications with carefully targeted individual consumers to obtain an immediate response, and cultivate lasting customer relationships

Direct marketing channel - A marketing channel that has no intermediary levels

Direct-mail marketing - Direct marketing through single mailings that include letters, ads, samples, foldouts, and other "salespeople with wings" sent to prospects on mailing lists

Discount - A straight reduction in price on purchases during a stated period of time

Electronic commerce (e-commerce) - The general term for a buying and selling process that is supported by electronic means

Employer Identification Number (EIN) - A unique nine-digit number assigned by the Internal Revenue Service (IRS) to businesses operating in the United States for the purposes of identification. Such number is required to open a bank account at a financial institution in the name of the business. This number can be obtained for free by visiting www.irs.gov

Entrepreneurship - A process by which people pursue opportunities, fulfilling needs and wants through innovation, without regard to the resources they currently control

Federal Insurance Contributions Act (FICA) - A United States payroll (or employment) tax imposed by the federal government on both employees and employers to fund Social Security and Medicare (federal programs that provide benefits for retirees, the disabled, and children of deceased workers). Social Security benefits include old-age, survivors, and disability insurance (OASDI). Medicare provides hospital insurance benefits

Fictitious Business Name (Doing Business As or "DBA") - This is a legal phrase in which the name of the business or operation does not include the owner's name, partners' names, or other identifying names. A DBA is required to open a bank account at a financial institution in the name of the business

Fixed costs - Costs that do not vary with production or sales level

Forecasting - The art of estimating future demand by anticipating what buyers are likely to do under a given set of conditions

Franchise - A contractual association between a manufacturer, wholesaler, or service organization (a franchiser) and independent businesspeople (franchisees) who buy the right to own and operate one or more units in the franchise system

Franchise organization - A contractual vertical marketing system in which a channel member, called a franchiser, links several stages in the production-distribution process

Functional discount - A price reduction offered by the seller to trade channel members who perform certain functions such as selling, storing, and recordkeeping

General need description - The stage in the business buying process in which the company describes the general characteristics and quantity of a needed item

Geographic segmentation - Dividing a market into different geographical units such as nations, states, regions, counties, cities, or neighborhoods

Gross margin - The amount of contribution to the business enterprise, after paying for direct fixed and variable unit costs (Gross Profit = Revenue − Cost of Goods Sold

Gross sales - The total amount that a company charges during a given period of time for merchandise

Group - Two or more people who interact to accomplish individual or mutual goals

Growth stage - The product life-cycle stage in which a product's sales start climbing quickly

Income segmentation - Dividing a market into different income groups

Indirect marketing channel - Channel containing one or more intermediary levels

Individual marketing - Tailoring products and marketing programs to the needs and preferences of individual customers. Individual marketing is also know as customized marketing, one-to-one marketing, and markets-of-one-marketing

Influencers - People in an organization's buying center who affect the buying decision. Influencers often help define specifications and also provide information for evaluating alternatives

Information search - The stage of the buyer decision process in which the consumer is aroused to search for more information. The consumer may simply have heightened attention or may go into active information search

Integrated direct marketing - Direct-marketing campaigns that use multiple vehicles and multiple stages to improve response rates and profits

Integrated marketing communications (IMC) - The concept under which a company carefully integrates and coordinates its many communications channels to deliver a clear, consistent, and compelling message about the organization and its products

Internal databases - Computerized collections of information obtained from data sources within the company

Internal marketing - Marketing by a service firm to train and effectively motivate its customer-contact employees and all the supporting service people to work as a team to provide customer satisfaction

Job description - A written statement of what a jobholder does, how it is done, and why it is done

Leading indicators - Time series that change in the same direction but in advance of company sales

Licensing - A method of entering a foreign market in which the company enters into an agreement with a licensee in the foreign market, offering the right to use a manufacturing process, trademark, patent, trade secret, or other item of value for a fee or royalty

Local marketing - Tailoring brands and promotions to the needs and wants of local customer groups (e.g. cities, neighborhoods, and even specific stores)

Macroenvironment - The larger societal forces that affect the microenvironment (i.e. demographic, economic, natural, technological, political, and cultural forces)

Markdown - A percentage reduction from the original selling price

Market - The set of all actual and potential buyers of a product or service

Market-centered company - A company that pays balanced attention to both customers and competitors in designing its marketing strategies

Market development - A strategy for company growth by identifying and developing new market segments for current company products

Market follower - A runner-up firm in an industry that wants to hold its share without rocking the boat

Market leader - The firm in an industry with the largest market share. The market leader usually leads other firms in price changes, new product introductions, distribution coverage, and promotion spending

Market penetration - A strategy for company growth by increasing sales of current products to current market segments without changing the product

Market-penetration pricing - Setting a low price for a new product in order to attract a large number of buyers and a large market share

Market positioning - Arranging for a product to occupy a clear, distinctive, and desirable place relative to competing products in the minds of target consumers. Formulating competitive positioning for a product and a detailed marketing mix

Market potential - The upper limit of market demand

Market segment - A group of consumers who respond in a similar way to a given set of marketing efforts

Market segmentation - Dividing a market into distinct groups of buyers on the basis of needs, characteristics, or behaviors who might require separate products or marketing mixes

Market-skimming pricing - Setting a high price for a new product to skim maximum revenues layer by layer from the segments willing to pay the high price. The company makes fewer but more profitable sales

Market targeting - The process of evaluating each market segment's attractiveness and selecting one or more segments to enter

Marketing - A social and managerial process whereby individuals and groups obtain what they need and want through creating and exchanging products and value with others

Marketing communications mix (promotion mix) - The specific mix of advertising, personal selling, sales promotion, public relations, and direct marketing a company uses to pursue its advertising and marketing objectives

Marketing control - The process of measuring and evaluating the results of marketing strategies and plans, and taking corrective action to ensure that marketing objectives are achieved

Marketing implementation - The process that turns marketing strategies and plans into marketing actions in order to accomplish strategic marketing objectives

Marketing intermediaries - Firms that help the company to promote, sell, and distribute its goods to final buyers. Marketing intermediaries include resellers, physical distribution firms, marketing service agencies, and financial intermediaries

Marketing management - The analysis, planning, implementation, and control of programs designed to create, build, and maintain beneficial exchanges with target buyers for the purpose of achieving organizational objectives

Marketing mix - The set of controllable tactical marketing tools (i.e. product, price, place, and promotion) that the firm blends to produce the response it wants in the target market

Marketing process - The process of (1)analyzing marketing opportunities, (2)selecting target markets, (3)developing the marketing mix, and (4)managing the marketing effort

Marketing research - The systematic design, collection, analysis, and reporting of data relevant to a specific marketing situation facing an organization

Markup - The percentage of the cost or price of a product added to the cost in order to arrive at a selling price

Microenvironment - The forces close to the company that affect its ability to serve its customers (e.g. the company, suppliers, marketing channel firms, customer markets, competitors, and publics)

Mission statement - A statement of the organization's purpose and what it wants to accomplish in the larger environment

Need - A state of felt deprivation

Need recognition - The first stage of the buyer decision process in which the consumer recognizes a problem or need

Niche marketing - Focusing on sub segments or niches with distinctive traits that may seek a special combination of benefits

Online ads - Ads that appear while subscribers are surfing online services or Web sites, including banners and pop-up windows

Online databases - Computerized collections of information available from online commercial sources or via the internet

Online marketing - Marketing conducted through interactive online computer systems, which link consumers with sellers electronically

Operating income - The amount of income left after reducing gross margin (sales minus cost of goods sold) by general operating expenses such as depreciation, selling, and administrative expenses

Opportunity - Positive external factors that a company can exploit

Packaging - The activities of designing and producing the container or wrapper for a product

Patronage reward - Cash or other award for the regular use of a certain company's products or services

Pay-back period - The time period at which the initial investment is fully recovered. This can be measured in days, months, or years

Perception - The process by which people select, organize, and interpret information to form a meaningful picture of the world

Personal selling - Personal presentation by the firm's sales force for the purpose of making sales and building customer relationships

Physical distribution (marketing logistics) - The tasks involved in planning, implementing, and controlling the physical flow of materials, final goods, and related information from points of origin to points of consumption to meet customer requirements at a profit

Point-of-purchase (POP) promotion - Display and demonstration that takes place at the point of purchase or sale

Premium - Good offered either free or at low cost as an incentive to buy a product

Presentation - The step in the selling process in which the salesperson tells the product "story" to the buyer, showing how the product will make or save money for the buyer

Price - The amount of money charged for a product or service, or the sum of the values that consumers exchange for the benefits of having or using the product or service

Price elasticity - A measure of the sensitivity of demand to changes in price

Price pack (cents-off deal) - Reduced price that is marked by the producer directly on the label or package

Primary demand - The level of total demand for all brands of a given product or service (e.g. the total demand for toothbrushes)

Product - Anything that can be offered to a market for attention, acquisition, use, or consumption that might satisfy a want or need. It includes physical objects, services, events, persons, places, organizations, and ideas

Product bundle pricing - Combining several products and offering the bundle at a reduced price

Product concept - The idea that consumers will favor products that offer the most quality, performance, and features and that the organization should therefore devote its energy to making continuous product improvements. A detailed version of the new product idea stated in meaningful consumer terms

Product development - A strategy for company growth by offering modified or new products to current market segments. Developing the product concept into a physical product in order to ensure that the product idea can be turned into a workable product

Product life cycle (PLC) - The course of a product's sales and profits over its lifetime. It involves five distinct stages: product development, introduction, growth, maturity, and decline

Product mix (or product assortment) - The set of all product lines and items that a particular seller offers for sale

Product position - The way the product is defined by consumers on important attributes (i.e. the place the product occupies in consumers' minds relative to competing products)

Product quality - The ability of a product to perform its functions, including the product's overall durability, reliability, precision, ease of operation and repair, and other valued attributes

Profit margin - The measure of profitability (Revenue / Net Income)

Promotional pricing - Temporarily pricing products below the list price, and sometimes even below cost, to increase short-run sales

Prospecting - The step in the selling process in which the salesperson identifies qualified potential customers

Psychographic segmentation - Dividing a market into different groups based on social class, lifestyle, or personality characteristics

Psychological pricing - A pricing approach that considers the psychology of prices and not simply the economics. The price is used to say something about the product

Public relations - Building good relations with the company's various publics by obtaining favorable publicity, building up a good image, and handling or heading off unfavorable rumors, stories, and events. Major PR tools include press relations, product publicity, corporate communications, lobbying, and public service

Push strategy - A promotion strategy that calls for using the sales force and trade promotion to push the product through channels. The producer promotes the product to wholesalers, the wholesalers promote to retailers, and the retailers promote to consumers

Quality - The totality of features and characteristics of a product or service that bear on its ability to satisfy stated or implied needs

Quantity discount - A price reduction to buyers who buy large volumes

Quick ratio (acid test ratio) - Measure of the business' liquidity, excluding inventory

Reference prices - Prices that buyers carry in their minds and refer to when they look at a given product

Relationship marketing - The process of creating, maintaining, and enhancing strong, value-laden relationships with customers and other stakeholders

Return on assets (ROA) - The Return on Assets (ROA) percentage shows how profitable a company's assets are in generating revenue

Return on equity (ROE) - Measures the rate of return on the ownership interest (shareholders' equity) of the common stock owners

Return on investment (ROI) - A common measure of managerial effectiveness (i.e. the ratio of net profit to investment)

Risk - Those conditions in which the decision maker is able t o estimate the likelihood of certain outcomes

Sales promotion - Short-term incentives to encourage the purchase or sale of a product or service

Sample - A segment of the population selected for marketing research to represent the population as a whole. A sample is typically a trial amount of the product

Seasonal discount - A price reduction to buyers who purchase merchandise or services out of season

Selling process - The steps that the salesperson follows when selling, which include prospecting and qualifying, pre-approach, approach, presentation and demonstration, handling objections, closing, and follow-up

Service - Any activity or benefit that one party can offer to another that is essentially intangible and does not result in the ownership of anything

Slotting fees - Payments demanded by retailers before they will accept new products and find available space (i.e. slots) for the products on the shelves

Social marketing - The design, implementation, and control of programs seeking to increase the acceptability of a social idea, cause, or practice among a target group

Societal marketing concept - The idea that the organization should determine the needs, wants, and interests of target markets and deliver the desired satisfactions more effectively and efficiently than do competitors in a way that maintains or improves the consumer's and society's well-being

Specialty product - Consumer product with unique characteristics or brand identification for which a significant group of buyers is willing to make a special purchase effort

Strategic planning - The process of developing and maintaining a strategic fit between the organization's goals and capabilities and its changing marketing opportunities. It involves defining a clear company mission, setting supporting objectives, designing a sound business portfolio, and coordinating functional strategies

Strengths - Activities the firm does well or resources it controls

Supplier search - The stage of the business buying process in which the buyer tries to find the best vendors

Supplier selection - The stage of the business buying process in which the buyer reviews proposals and selects a supplier

Target market - A set of buyers sharing common needs or characteristics that the company decides to serve

Team selling - Using teams of people from sales, marketing, engineering, finance, technical support, and even upper management to service large, complex accounts

Test marketing - The stage of new product development in which the product and marketing program are tested in more realistic market settings

Third-party logistics provider - An independent logistics provider that performs any or all of the functions required to get its customers' product to market

Threat - Negative external environmental factors that a company cannot exploit

Total costs - The sum of the fixed and variable costs for any given level of production

Total customer cost - The total of all the monetary, time, energy, and psychic costs associated with a marketing offer

Total market demand - The total volume of a product or service that would be bought by a defined consumer group in a defined geographic area in a defined time period in a defined marketing environment under a defined level and mix of industry marketing effort

Uniform-delivered pricing - A geographical pricing strategy in which the company charges the same price plus freight to all customers, regardless of their location

Users - Members of the organization who will use the product or service. Users often initiate the buying proposal and help define product specifications

Value analysis - An approach to cost reduction in which components are studied carefully to determine if they can be redesigned, standardized, or made by less costly methods of production

Value-based pricing - Setting price based on buyers' perceptions of value rather than on the seller's cost

Value pricing - Offering just the right combination of quality and good service at a fair price

Variable costs - Costs that vary directly with the level of production

Want - The form taken by a human need as shaped by culture and individual personality

Weaknesses - Activities the firm does not do well or resources it needs but does not possess

<u>Wholesaling</u> - All activities involved in selling goods and services to those buying for resale or business use

<u>Word-of-mouth influence</u> - Personal communication about a product between target buyers and neighbors, friends, family members, and associates

Made in the USA
Lexington, KY
18 June 2010